KING
ARTHUR

KING ARTHUR

Paul C. Doherty

1987
CHELSEA HOUSE PUBLISHERS
NEW YORK
NEW HAVEN   PHILADELPHIA

EDITORIAL DIRECTOR: Nancy Toff
SENIOR EDITOR: John W. Selfridge
ASSOCIATE EDITOR: Marian W. Taylor
MANAGING EDITOR: Karyn Gullen Browne
COPY CHIEF: Perry King
EDITORIAL STAFF: Maria Behan, Karen Dreste,
　　　　　　　　Pierre Hauser, Kathleen McDermott,
　　　　　　　　Alma Rodriguez-Sokol, Howard Ratner,
　　　　　　　　Bert Yaeger
PICTURE EDITOR: Elizabeth Terhune
PICTURE RESEARCH: Susan B. Hamburger
ART DIRECTOR: Giannella Garrett
LAYOUT: Irene Friedman
ART ASSISTANTS: Noreen Lamb, Carol McDougall,
　　　　　　　　Victoria Tomaselli
COVER ILLUSTRATION: Richard Leonard

Frontispiece courtesy of Scala/Art Resource

First Printing

Library of Congress Cataloging in Publication Data

Doherty, Paul. KING ARTHUR.

(World leaders past & present)
Bibliography: p.
Includes index.
1. Arthur, King—Juvenile literature. 2. Great Britain—
Kings and rulers—Biography—Juvenile literature. 3. Great
Britain—History—Anglo-Saxon period, 449–1066—Juvenile
literature. 4. Arthurian romances—History and criticism—
Juvenile literature.
[1. Arthur, King. 2. Kings, queens, rulers, etc. 3. Great
Britain—History—Anglo-Saxon period, 449–1066]
I. Title. II. Series.
DA152.5.A7D67   1986   942.01′4 [B] [92] 86-20739

ISBN 0-87754-506-5

Chelsea House Publishers

Contents

CHELSEA HOUSE PUBLISHERS

WORLD LEADERS PAST & PRESENT

ON LEADERSHIP
Arthur M. Schlesinger, jr.

LEADERSHIP, it may be said, is really what makes the world go round. Love no doubt smooths the passage; but love is a private transaction between consenting adults. Leadership is a public transaction with history. The idea of leadership affirms the capacity of individuals to move, inspire, and mobilize masses of people so that they act together in pursuit of an end. Sometimes leadership serves good purposes, sometimes bad; but whether the end is benign or evil, great leaders are those men and women who leave their personal stamp on history.

Now, the very concept of leadership implies the proposition that individuals can make a difference. This proposition has never been universally accepted. From classical times to the present day, eminent thinkers have regarded individuals as no more than the agents and pawns of larger forces, whether the gods and goddesses of the ancient world or, in the modern era, race, class, nation, the dialectic, the will of the people, the spirit of the times, history itself. Against such forces, the individual dwindles into insignificance.

So contends the thesis of historical determinism. Tolstoy's great novel *War and Peace* offers a famous statement of the case. Why, Tolstoy asked, did millions of men in the Napoleonic wars, denying their human feelings and their common sense, move back and forth across Europe slaughtering their fellows? "The war," Tolstoy answered, "was bound to happen simply because it was bound to happen." All prior history predetermined it. As for leaders, they, Tolstoy said, "are but the labels that serve to give a name to an end and, like labels, they have the least possible connection with the event." The greater the leader, "the more conspicuous the inevitability and the predestination of every act he commits." The leader, said Tolstoy, is "the slave of history."

Determinism takes many forms. Marxism is the determinism of class. Nazism the determinism of race. But the idea of men and women as the slaves of history runs athwart the deepest human instincts. Rigid determinism abolishes the idea of human freedom—

the assumption of free choice that underlies every move we make, every word we speak, every thought we think. It abolishes the idea of human responsibility, since it is manifestly unfair to reward or punish people for actions that are by definition beyond their control. No one can live consistently by any deterministic creed. The Marxist states prove this themselves by their extreme susceptibility to the cult of leadership.

More than that, history refutes the idea that individuals make no difference. In December 1931 a British politician crossing Park Avenue in New York City between 76th and 77th Streets around 10:30 P.M. looked in the wrong direction and was knocked down by an automobile—a moment, he later recalled, of a man aghast, a world aglare: "I do not understand why I was not broken like an eggshell or squashed like a gooseberry." Fourteen months later an American politician, sitting in an open car in Miami, Florida, was fired on by an assassin; the man beside him was hit. Those who believe that individuals make no difference to history might well ponder whether the next two decades would have been the same had Mario Constasino's car killed Winston Churchill in 1931 and Giuseppe Zangara's bullet killed Franklin Roosevelt in 1933. Suppose, in addition, that Adolf Hitler had been killed in the street fighting during the Munich *Putsch* of 1923 and that Lenin had died of typhus during World War I. What would the 20th century be like now?

For better or for worse, individuals do make a difference. "The notion that a people can run itself and its affairs anonymously," wrote the philosopher William James, "is now well known to be the silliest of absurdities. Mankind does nothing save through initiatives on the part of inventors, great or small, and imitation by the rest of us—these are the sole factors in human progress. Individuals of genius show the way, and set the patterns, which common people then adopt and follow."

Leadership, James suggests, means leadership in thought as well as in action. In the long run, leaders in thought may well make the greater difference to the world. But, as Woodrow Wilson once said, "Those only are leaders of men, in the general eye, who lead in action. . . . It is at their hands that new thought gets its translation into the crude language of deeds." Leaders in thought often invent in solitude and obscurity, leaving to later generations the tasks of imitation. Leaders in action—the leaders portrayed in this series—have to be effective in their own time.

And they cannot be effective by themselves. They must act in response to the rhythms of their age. Their genius must be adapted, in a phrase of William James's, "to the receptivities of the moment." Leaders are useless without followers. "There goes the mob," said the French politician hearing a clamor in the streets. "I am their leader. I must follow them." Great leaders turn the inchoate emotions of the mob to purposes of their own. They seize on the opportunities of their time, the hopes, fears, frustrations, crises, potentialities. They succeed when events have prepared the way for them, when the community is awaiting to be aroused, when they can provide the clarifying and organizing ideas. Leadership ignites the circuit between the individual and the mass and thereby alters history.

It may alter history for better or for worse. Leaders have been responsible for the most extravagant follies and most monstrous crimes that have beset suffering humanity. They have also been vital in such gains as humanity has made in individual freedom, religious and racial tolerance, social justice and respect for human rights.

There is no sure way to tell in advance who is going to lead for good and who for evil. But a glance at the gallery of men and women in *World Leaders—Past and Present* suggests some useful tests.

One test is this: do leaders lead by force or by persuasion? By command or by consent? Through most of history leadership was exercised by the divine right of authority. The duty of followers was to defer and to obey. "Theirs not to reason why,/ Theirs but to do and die." On occasion, as with the so-called "enlightened despots" of the 18th century in Europe, absolutist leadership was animated by humane purposes. More often, absolutism nourished the passion for domination, land, gold and conquest and resulted in tyranny.

The great revolution of modern times has been the revolution of equality. The idea that all people should be equal in their legal condition has undermined the old structure of authority, hierarchy and deference. The revolution of equality has had two contrary effects on the nature of leadership. For equality, as Alexis de Tocqueville pointed out in his great study *Democracy in America*, might mean equality in servitude as well as equality in freedom.

"I know of only two methods of establishing equality in the political world," Tocqueville wrote. "Rights must be given to every citizen, or none at all to anyone . . . save one, who is the master of all." There was no middle ground "between the sovereignty of all and the absolute power of one man." In his astonishing prediction of 20th-century totalitarian dictatorship, Tocqueville explained how the revolution of equality could lead to the *"Führerprinzip"* and more terrible absolutism than the world had ever known.

But when rights are given to every citizen and the sovereignty of all is established, the problem of leadership takes a new form, becomes more exacting than ever before. It is easy to issue commands and enforce them by the rope and the stake, the concentration camp and the *gulag.* It is much harder to use argument and achievement to overcome opposition and win consent. The Founding Fathers of the United States understood the difficulty. They believed that history had given them the opportunity to decide, as Alexander Hamilton wrote in the first Federalist Paper, whether men are indeed capable of basing government on "reflection and choice, or whether they are forever destined to depend . . . on accident and force."

Government by reflection and choice called for a new style of leadership and a new quality of followership. It required leaders to be responsive to popular concerns, and it required followers to be active and informed participants in the process. Democracy does not eliminate emotion from politics; sometimes it fosters demagoguery; but it is confident that, as the greatest of democratic leaders put it, you cannot fool all of the people all of the time. It measures leadership by results and retires those who overreach or falter or fail.

It is true that in the long run despots are measured by results too. But they can postpone the day of judgment, sometimes indefinitely, and in the meantime they can do infinite harm. It is also true that democracy is no guarantee of virtue and intelligence in government, for the voice of the people is not necessarily the voice of God. But democracy, by assuring the right of opposition, offers built-in resistance to the evils inherent in absolutism. As the theologian Reinhold Niebuhr summed it up, "Man's capacity for justice makes democracy possible, but man's inclination to injustice makes democracy necessary."

A second test for leadership is the end for which power is sought. When leaders have as their goal the supremacy of a master race or the promotion of totalitarian revolution or the acquisition and exploitation of colonies or the protection of greed and privilege or the preservation of personal power, it is likely that their leadership will do little to advance the cause of humanity. When their goal is the abolition of slavery, the liberation of women, the enlargement of opportunity for the poor and powerless, the extension of equal rights to racial minorities, the defense of the freedoms of expression and opposition, it is likely that their leadership will increase the sum of human liberty and welfare.

Leaders have done great harm to the world. They have also conferred great benefits. You will find both sorts in this series. Even "good" leaders must be regarded with a certain wariness. Leaders are not demigods; they put on their trousers one leg after another just like ordinary mortals. No leader is infallible, and every leader needs to be reminded of this at regular intervals. Irreverence irritates leaders but is their salvation. Unquestioning submission corrupts leaders and demands followers. Making a cult of a leader is always a mistake. Fortunately hero worship generates its own antidote. "Every hero," said Emerson, "becomes a bore at last."

The signal benefit the great leaders confer is to embolden the rest of us to live according to our own best selves, to be active, insistent, and resolute in affirming our own sense of things. For great leaders attest to the reality of human freedom against the supposed inevitabilities of history. And they attest to the wisdom and power that may lie within the most unlikely of us, which is why Abraham Lincoln remains the supreme example of great leadership. A great leader, said Emerson, exhibits new possibilities to all humanity. "We feed on genius. . . . Great men exist that there may be greater men."

Great leaders, in short, justify themselves by emancipating and empowering their followers. So humanity struggles to master its destiny, remembering with Alexis de Tocqueville: "It is true that around every man a fatal circle is traced beyond which he cannot pass; but within the wide verge of that circle he is powerful and free; as it is with man, so with communities."

—*New York*

1

Birth of a Hero

"There was seen in the churchyard, against the high altar, a great stone four square, like unto marble stone, and in the midst thereof was like an anvil of steel a foot on high, and therein stuck a fair sword . . . and letters there were written in gold about the sword that saiden thus: WHOSO PULLETH OUT THIS SWORD OF THIS STONE AND ANVIL, IS RIGHTWISE KING BORN OF ALL ENGLAND."

After Christmas Mass in the greatest church in London, all claimants to the throne gathered about. One after another they gave the sword a pull, but none of those assembled could remove it. " 'He is not here,' said the archbishop, 'that shall achieve the sword, but no doubt God will make him known.' " He then declared that the next contender for the sword in the stone must be victorious at a combat of arms.

Thus was a great tournament arranged for New Year's Day. Horses charged on the hard earth bearing their lance-wielding masters in jousts, while elsewhere swords crashed against shields as the knights fought on foot. To this test of strength arrived Ector and his son Kay, a knight who wished to try his luck in combat, and Arthur, his squire. But Kay had lost his sword and Arthur was sent to fetch him one.

The boy said to himself, "I will ride to the churchyard, and take the sword with me that sticketh in

Whither has not the flying fame spread and familiarized the name of Arthur the Briton, ever as far as the Empire of Christendom extends?
—ALAIN DE LILLE
12th-century French philosopher and poet

As onlookers gather, young Arthur prepares to pull the sword from the stone and anvil. Upon drawing forth the blade and thus passing the wizard Merlin's magical test, Arthur would be proclaimed king of England.

THE STORY OF KING ARTHUR AND HIS KNIGHTS, H. PYLE, SCRIBNER'S

the stone, for my brother Sir Kay shall not be without a sword this day." Grasping the sword around the handles, he "lightly and fiercely" pulled it from the stone, and rode back to deliver the sword to Kay.

Later, Arthur repeated this feat before all who had gathered. On learning of this miracle, they all fell to their knees and cried, "We will have Arthur unto our king, . . . for we all see that it is God's will that he shall be our king." Thus, Arthur was proclaimed king of England.

The legend of the sword in the stone is perhaps the most famous of the many legends surrounding the greatest of all British kings — King Arthur. But, who was Arthur? Did he really exist? Why is he the most celebrated figure of all medieval literature?

Our search begins in that western part of Britain known as Wales. The time is around the year 600. A bard, or medieval poet, is singing of a valiant, but recently slain, warrior. He describes this great warrior in glowing verse, yet, while detailing the hero's military prowess, the bard admits that he was not the best: "But he was not Arthur." The bard's poem, the *Gododdin*, which was written down later in the century, is famous just because of that indirect reference. Although some historians believe that the phrase was added later to the manuscript of the poem, most believe it is original. If so, it is the first mention of the legendary King Arthur. The phrase does not provide much information, but something can be made from this historical reference.

For the comparison "But he was not Arthur" to have made any sense to the poet's audience, Arthur must have been so well-known that a simple mention of his name would be enough for listeners to recall exploits of Arthur's valor and heroism. Second, it is clear that Arthur was famous not only because he was a king or ruler, but because he was a warrior, a fighter, evidently the most renowned of his time. Third, since Arthur was already famous at the time of this poem, a figure against whom all other warriors could be compared, he must have lived some time before 600, but probably not so far before that date that his memory was not fresh in the mind of this poet and his audience. Finally, we

MYSTERIES OF THE WORLD, ED. CHRISTOPHER RICKS, CHARTWELL BOOKS

At a joust, armor-clad knights menacingly brandish their swords after throwing away their lances, broken on an ineffective first charge. Warriors and spectators often traveled great distances to attend these tournaments of strength, courage, and honor. It was in such events that Arthur's adoptive brother Sir Kay participated.

An illustration from a medieval manuscript depicting Arthur's coronation. Most of the facts attributed to the Arthur of history were derived from early works of literature. These books were often simple chronicles written by the few literate men of the era, particularly monks such as Gildas and Nennius.

must take into account the normal practices of Welsh poets at this time. We expect that modern poets and novelists will describe characters who are fictitious, resembling real persons, but still the products of their authors' imaginations. In earlier times, this was not the practice. Historians believe that all of the characters in the early poems of the Welsh people, poems such as the *Gododdin*, appear to be real persons, and that the events in those poems are equally real.

So Arthur appears to have actually lived. It is important to keep that point in mind, for his existence has been disputed. And the phrase "But he was not Arthur" reveals a great deal to us. It seems to tell us that we are dealing with a historical person, a warrior who left his mark on his people.

If we wish to know why Arthur became so great a hero to the British people, we must seek to understand the crisis that Britain underwent in the 6th century, the time in which Arthur probably lived. One historian calls the Age of Arthur the beginning of modern British history, and all historians, even those who doubt the importance of Arthur, recognize the critical importance of this period.

Until just before the time of Arthur, the island of Britain had been a province of the vast Roman Empire. "Britannia" was its Roman name, and although it was the northernmost frontier of the empire, it had been occupied by Roman soldiers since the middle of the 1st century. But now, in the 5th century, the power of Rome's empire was weakening everywhere.

An invading army of German tribesmen called Visigoths, driven by scarcity of food and threat of invasion by Asiatic tribes, left their eastern European homelands. They settled peacefully for a short time in the eastern part of the Roman Empire, but soon revolted against the imperial government. Under the leadership of Alaric, they moved south along the coastline of Italy. In 410 the invaders captured Rome, the capital city of the empire. Although the Visigoths did not remain to occupy the imperial city, Alaric's invasion exposed the military weakness of the Roman Empire. Before the end of the century

> *Arthur long upheld the sinking state, and raised the broken spirit of his countrymen to war.*
> —WILLIAM OF MALMESBURY
> 12th-century British historian

both city and empire would fall.

During the years just preceding Alaric's invasion of the imperial city, soldiers stationed in Britannia had been recalled to prepare to defend the threatened homeland. Partly because of their efforts in defending the empire abroad, the Britons had become less and less able to defend themselves at home. They appealed for protection to the Roman emperor, Honorius, who was no longer in Rome, but in the city of Ravenna, where his court had moved to escape the Visigoth invasion. The reply that they received from Honorius is not surprising: "Let the colonies look to their own defense."

These people who had been conquered by the Romans and who were now being told to prepare for their own defense were called Britons. Their predecessors, the Celts, had migrated from the continent to Britain and Ireland more than 500 years before the Roman invasion. They almost certainly owed their success in conquering the inhabitants whom they found on the island to the one great advantage that they held. The Celts were extremely advanced in their knowledge of how to forge iron; the people defeated by the Celts had little knowledge of ironworking. The iron weapons of the Celts made them more formidable warriors, and their iron farming implements made them more capable farmers. They easily dominated the land to which they had migrated.

The Celts were not a single nation, however, but a collection of independent tribes, each ruled by its own king and queen. Each tribe had an aristocracy, as well as slaves. Each tribe also had a class, called druids, who served both as the priests and judges of the tribe. The Celtic women shared duties, including military leadership, with the men. Sometimes the Celtic tribes lived together, peacefully; sometimes they were at war. When the Romans arrived, some tribes welcomed them, others resisted them.

But the Celtic tribes who resisted the Romans in the 1st century were no match for the soldiers of the Roman legions. Roman soldiers were better trained, supplied, and organized, and more adapt-

On becoming emperor of Rome in the 2nd century A.D., the successful administrator and commander Hadrian made two tours of the imperial frontier colony of Britannia. In 122 he provided for the protection of Rome's northernmost colony by ordering the construction of Hadrian's Wall.

19

able than those of any previous army. A Roman legion consisted of 10 cohorts, each with 555 men. Individual soldiers were armed with swords and spears, and protected by shields. The artillery consisted of giant crossbows and catapults. The well-trained soldiers were fit and flexible, not only for warfare, but for building the roads, bridges, and towns that aided their military campaigns and then established them as rulers of the island. Their network of roads, which crisscrossed the island, permitted not only the swift movement of troops and supplies, but greater trade and better communications as well. The greatest surviving Roman landmark in Britain is the wall named for the Emperor Hadrian. Built between Scotland and England as a defense against the northern Picts, fierce enemies

Hadrian's Wall, stretching almost 75 miles across Britain from the Solway Firth on the west coast to the mouth of the Tyne River on the east, was built by the Romans in an effort to repel the invasions of the wild Pictish warriors of Scotland. Much of the wall still remains today.

of the Romans, the wall stretches from the Irish Sea to the North Sea, a distance of about 75 miles.

But the Romans were not only able warriors; they were able governors of conquered people as well. One of the characteristics of Roman rule was that the native populations played central roles in the defense and governance of the country. Also, it was Roman policy to encourage soldiers whose years of military service were over to settle in the country in which they had served. Inevitably, during the course of the four centuries in which the Romans ruled Britannia, the difference between natives and conquerors, between the Celts and Romans, became blurred, giving rise to people who called themselves Britons.

This blurring may be better understood if we re-

Covered from head-to-toe with blue paint and tattoos, Pictish warriors were fierce opposition for the Roman troops stationed in Britain. Although inferior to the Romans in training and weaponry, the Picts' ferocity and superior numbers often led them to victory.

alize that the Roman Empire was never a nation in the modern sense. Its citizens were bound neither by race nor geography. Their bond was forged by their common official language, Latin; by their common system of law; and by their common style of governing. Taken together, these common traditions and skills may be called a civilization.

The Roman conquest brought a higher standard of life to Celtic Britain. It is also true, however, that in many ways Celtic culture provided a ready basis for the addition of Roman civilization. The Celtic earth and timber hill-forts, built originally for defense, developed in many cases into the towns that were the center of Roman administration and trade. The Celtic religion, overseen by the druids, was compatible with Christianity, which the Romans brought. Both religions encompassed not only worship, which is common to all religions, but a belief in immortality and a moral code of conduct as well. Thus, although the Romans could no longer provide military support for Britain, the withdrawal of their army hardly ended the influence of their civilization, which had been the basis of British life for nearly four centuries.

But certainly, the withdrawal of the Roman forces opened Britain to enemies from all sides. The British population of mixed Celtic and Roman stock was destined to be conquered by yet another invading people. Because their membership in the Roman Empire had ensured their peace for centuries, the Britons were poorly prepared to defend themselves. From Ireland, the island to the west of Britain, came tribes of Celts who had never been subjected to Roman rule. From Scotland in the north came other Celts and Picts. From the continent of Europe came three groups rather similar in their Germanic origin and culture, the Saxons, the Angles, and the Jutes.

Of all these groups, it was the Saxons who posed the greatest danger. Skilled seamen, they raided the coastal towns of south and east Britain and moved inland along its rivers. Their original goal was to plunder, but by 450 their bases along the southeastern coast of Britain had become permanent settlements. Roman civilization was giving way to

It is of this Arthur that the Britons fondly tell so many fables, even to the present day: a man to be celebrated not by idle fictions but by authentic history.
—WILLIAM OF MALMESBURY
12th-century British historian

tribal life, and Christianity to pagan gods.

The strongest of the British leaders during the years immediately following the withdrawal of Roman soldiers appears to have been Vortigern, a chieftain from Wales. It is believed that Vortigern had never lived under the direct influence of Rome and Christianity, but had proven useful to the empire during its last years of rule in Britain when he served as a frontier auxiliary, someone who could help keep peace along the border. Following the withdrawal of Rome, and as a result of a series of political alliances and military conquests, Vortigern controlled large areas of Britain.

The situation that faced him was a desperate one. A historian of the time, who feared the worst, describes the scene:

> The Romans having now withdrawn their forces and abandoned Britain, the whole frame of affairs fell into disorder and misery. . . . There descend in great crowds, from the little narrow bores of their Carroghes or Carts, wherein they were brought over the Scitick [Scottish] vale, about the middle of summer, in a scorching hot season, a dusking swarm of vermin, or hideous crew of Scots and Picts, somewhat different in manners but alike in thirsting after blood; who, finding that their [the Britons] old confederates [the Romans] were marched home, and refused to return any more, put on greater boldness than ever and possessed themselves of the North. To withstand this invasion, the towers [along Hadrian's Wall] are defended by a lazy garrison, undisciplined, and too cowardly to engage an enemy; being enfeebled with continual sloth and idleness. In the meanwhile the naked enemy advance with their own hooked weapons by which the miserable Britains, pulled down from the tops of walls, are dashed against the ground. To those that were destroyed after this manner, had this advantage in an untimely death, that they escaped these miserable sufferings which immediately befell their brothers and children.

It was the threat of these Picts and Scots that

Vortigern feared most. For this reason, he made a treaty with the Jute leaders, Hengist and Horsa. He gave to the Jutes, Angles, and Saxons more territory in the southeast of Britain where they had already settled, and agreed to pay them tribute money each year. In return they promised to assist Vortigern in his campaigns against the northern invaders.

Vortigern's treaty was short-lived. Peace was restored, but after a few years, the three southern tribes — the Saxons, Angles, and Jutes — each demanded more land. Vortigern was willing to give them the land but, in exchange, he sought a re-

Mithras, the god of heroes and soldiers, was a favorite among Roman legionnaires throughout the empire. Although the Romans withdrew from Britain in the late 4th century, this form of hero worship had already greatly influenced the Britons. Some historians believe that King Arthur himself might have been a worshipper of Mithras.

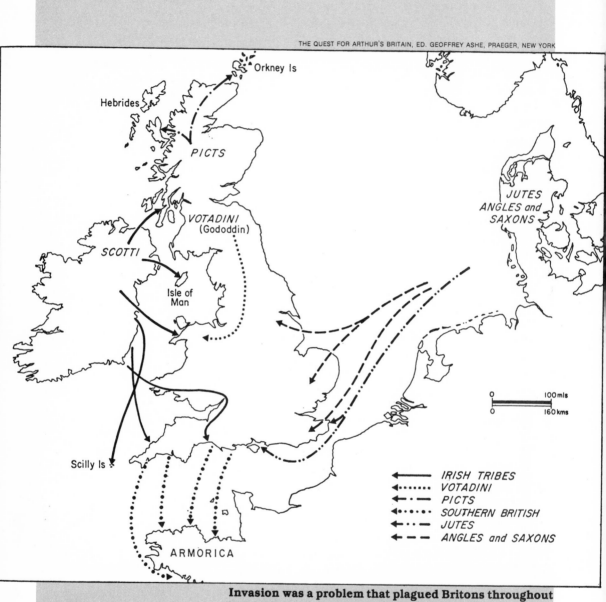

THE QUEST FOR ARTHUR'S BRITAIN, ED. GEOFFREY ASHE, PRAEGER, NEW YORK

Orkney Is

Hebrides

PICTS

VOTADINI
(Gododdin)

SCOTTI

Isle of
Man

Scilly Is

ARMORICA

JUTES
ANGLES and
SAXONS

| 0 | | | 100 mls |
| 0 | | | 160 kms |

→ IRISH TRIBES
◄······ VOTADINI
◄·—·— PICTS
◄·····•· SOUTHERN BRITISH
◄··—·· JUTES
◄— — — ANGLES and SAXONS

Invasion was a problem that plagued Britons throughout
history. The numerous attacks made by the Saxons, Angles, and Jutes from northern Europe in the 4th to 6th
centuries helped unite the Britons in opposition.

duction in the amount of tribute that he was paying to Hengist and Horsa in return for keeping peace. This condition proved unacceptable and the treaty broke down. Vortigern's effectiveness as a leader ended. The Saxons once again began plundering the areas near where they had settled. Within a quarter of a century after the Romans had withdrawn from the island, the Saxons were vying for control of all Britain.

Leadership of the Britons was now taken up by Ambrosius, whose kingdom in the southwest of Britain had existed independent of Vortigern's rule. Ambrosius differed from Vortigern in two ways, which would prove to be important. First, he was very much influenced by the old Roman ways of organization and fighting. He may himself have been from a Roman family that lived in Britain. Second, his soldiers were, like him, Christians. Christianity had come to Britain in the 2nd century, and although many of the inhabitants of the island were still pagans, people who believed in many gods, in Vortigern's time, the aristocracy, the group most influenced by Roman civilization, appears to have been mostly Christian. Certainly Ambrosius would not make Vortigern's mistake and trust the defense of Britain to pagan mercenaries.

It is possible to contrast in the broadest terms these opposing forces — the defending Britons, led by Ambrosius, and the advancing Saxons, Angles, and Jutes, led by Hengist. The small army of Ambrosius relied upon the central organization, disciplined training, and the cavalry that the Romans had introduced. The Britons fought, however, only because they had to, their purpose was to end the threat to the Roman way of life, which had brought them peace, prosperity, and a common purpose. These people were engaged in a war of liberation. Their enemies, on the other hand, more numerous but not centrally organized, went into battle as families and tribes. Their loyalty was to their kin, and they fought with ferocity — the only failure they understood was the disgrace of not fighting to the end. They fought because they wished to, and the reward they sought was to enrich themselves through plunder and pillage. They had no intention of developing a nation or a settled way of life; for them the immediate goal of self-enrichment was everything. Finally, as Christians, many of the Britons believed that life in this world was a mere preparation for the eternal life to come. The Britons' enemies were pagans, and they believed that people must live their lives to the fullest.

It appears that Ambrosius had early success in battle. He defeated and killed the enemy leader, Hengist, and for a time kept the Saxons and their allies confined to the southeast corner of the island. But there was no certain peace. The exact happenings at this time are unclear, for one consequence of the withdrawal of Roman forces was that written records of the subsequent years are very scarce. We may safely believe, however, that there were forays by the Saxons along the southern coast and into the center of Britain, and these often were met by resistance from the Britons.

One of these battles, Badon, is recalled as the most significant. Although the actual location of Badon Hill is disputed, it was certainly in the west of Britain, and for the Saxons to have traveled there for battle would have required a combined effort of a number of their tribes. We may assume that the Saxons undertook this effort because they felt confident that their ferocity and superior numbers would allow them to win a victory deep in the British stronghold. They were wrong. According to one version of the battle, the Saxons, after besieging the hilltop fortress of the Britons for three days, emerged from their cover and were routed by the British cavalry.

In one sense, the Battle of Badon is of little significance. The Saxon occupation of Britain was not stopped, only delayed for a few decades. After their decisive defeat, the Saxons abandoned their attempts to take control of Britain for 40 years. By the end of the 6th century, however, most of Britain would be under the control of these invaders, the Anglo-Saxons, as we have come to call them, and from one of these tribes, the Angles, comes our present name for the inhabitants of Britain, the English.

Without the Roman legions to protect them the Britons
were vulnerable to attack from numerous enemies. In
order to repel attacks by the Scots and Picts from the
north, the British chieftain Vortigern made a defense
treaty with Hengist and Horsa, the leaders of the Saxon
and Jute invaders.

2

The Early Chronicles

At a time when the land was being overrun with invaders and a way of life was being threatened, Arthur came to symbolize the British resistance. He was a great hero for his times. And the single event that marked the greatness of the resistance was the Battle of Badon. It stemmed the Anglo-Saxon tide for a while, and in the minds of his people it must have been one of history's greatest events.

The existence of the Battle of Badon can be verified by the writings of the Welsh monk and historian, Gildas. His book, which was written around 540, only a few decades after the Battle of Badon, is called *Concerning the Ruin and Conquest of Britain.* In his own words it is a "complaining book." His constant lament is that the disasters that the British people suffered at the hands of the Anglo-Saxons after the Roman withdrawal were clear evidence that God was punishing them for their sins. Furthermore, he wrote, if the Britons did not reform their lives, the punishment would lead to their destruction. It is in the course of this judgment that Gildas describes the Battle of Badon, and the four decades of peace that followed it.

For the historian of Arthur, however, there is a

Arthur, the greatest of all poetical subjects . . .
—ALFRED, LORD TENNYSON
19th-century British poet

King Arthur as depicted in the Tapestry of the Nine Christian Worthies (or Heroes). Since most of the chronicles of King Arthur and his era were written by monks, the king early on became associated with Christianity.

THE METROPOLITAN MUSEUM OF ART, THE CLOISTERS COLLECTION, MENSEY FUND, 1932

curious feature in Gildas's account of these events. Unlike most of the later historians he does not name Arthur as the commander of the British forces at Badon; in fact, he does not directly credit the victory to any particular leader. Gildas does state, however, that Ambrosius led his warriors in a series of battles that culminated with Badon Hill, thereby implying that Ambrosius was responsible for the victory.

For historians who believe not only that Arthur existed but that he was a figure of considerable importance, this fact requires explanation. Why did Gildas, the historian most nearly a contemporary of Arthur, not credit him with the great victory at Ba-

HISTOIRE DE LA LITTÉRATURE FRANÇAISE ILLUSTRÉE, J. BEDIER, LAROUSSE, PARIS

don? Explanations may be found by considering Gildas's purpose in writing. He did not set out to construct a historical narrative, but rather a sermon to invoke repentance for past sins. His work, therefore, only gives a brief survey of the persons and events of the time. Also, since Gildas wished to scold his readers into leading passive, moral lives, it would hardly have served his purpose to pay special attention to Arthur, who in the few decades between the Battle of Badon and the writing of *Concerning the Ruin and Conquest of Britain*, was being celebrated in the songs of bards as the greatest hero of British history.

The history of King Arthur is invariably filled with descriptions of warriors in combat. Here two knights boast of their victories, each one represented by a sword.

Arthur was first attributed with leading the British victory two centuries after the event. Writing around 800, the Welsh monk and historian Nennius mentioned Badon as one of Arthur's many military victories. Nennius, like other historians of his time, began his history at the creation of the world and carried it forward to his own time. His sources were the writings of others — most of them lost, and known to us only because Nennius borrowed them — and he appears to have been very faithful to these sources. He did not use his sources as a later historian might, evaluating them and arranging them in order to demonstrate some specific purpose. Nennius was apparently satisfied merely to set down, in what he believed to be chronological order, everything that he could learn about the history of the world. He quaintly summarized his method: "I have made a heap of all I found."

In this heap is the first direct reference to Arthur. According to Nennius, Arthur fought against the Saxons *cum regibus Brittonum, sed ipse dux erat bellorum.* That is, Arthur fought "alongside the kings of the Britons, but it was he that was the battle leader." Nennius goes on to credit him with victories in 12 battles:

> The first battle was at the mouth of the river which is called Glein. The next four were on the banks of another river, which is called Dubglas and is in the region Linnius. The sixth was upon the river which is called Basses. The seventh was in the wood of Celidon; that is, Cat Coit Celidon. The eighth was by Castle Guinnion, in which Arthur carried on his shoulders an image of St. Mary Ever Virgin, and there was a great slaughter of them through the strength of Our Lord Jesus Christ and of the Virgin Mary his maiden-mother. The ninth was in the city of the Legion. The tenth was on the river which is called Tribuit. The eleventh was on a hill called Agned. The twelfth was on Mount Badon, in which — on that day — there fell in one onslaught of Arthur's, nine hundred and sixty men; and none slew them but he alone, and in all his battles he remained victor.

The same kind of questions can be asked of Nen-

"Blessed Mary Ever Virgin" and the Christ child adorned the shield of King Arthur according to this illustration from a medieval manuscript. The belief that God protected the king was commonly found in the works of the chroniclers of early Britain.

nius that were asked of the poet who composed the *Gododdin*. What can be inferred from the information that is presented? First of all, the source for this description of Arthur's victories was probably a poem sung by Welsh bards. The Welsh language was an oral, not a written one; it had no alphabet. During these centuries all accounts were written in Latin, and the only persons who knew how to write were priests and monks. In the absence of a written language, the songs of the bards constituted all that most of the inhabitants of Britain knew of the history of their people. Historians can even identify the kind of poem it was that Nennius was using as his source. It was a "battle-listing," a type of story that appears to have been a Welsh favorite. Although we cannot be sure when the poem that was Nennius's source was composed, historians believe that it was an old one, probably having first been sung 300 years before Nennius wrote his history. This belief is based on the fact that none of the battle sites to which Nennius refers can be pinpointed. If the poem had been composed nearer to the time when Nennius wrote, or if Nennius had given his own name to the battle sites, modern historians would most probably be able to identify the locations. But, in fact, historians disagree widely about the locations. Some of them doubt that Arthur could have been the British commander at all 12 battles. And still others, who believe that some of the battle sites are in the north of England, not in the west, have gone further, and have speculated not only that there must have been more than one Arthur, but that these "Arthurs" were not Welsh, but Scottish.

But the list does provide us with some possibilities for agreement. First, most of the battles were fought at rivers. This is plausible enough. Rivers were barriers that kept groups of people apart, except at those places where they could be forded (crossed by foot). Consequently, fords in rivers are frequent battle sites, one army trying to cross, the other trying to prevent its crossing. Second, Nennius's Arthur is clearly a Christian king. Although he probably carried the image of the "Blessed Mary Ever Virgin" on his shield, not on his shoulders as

Nennius has it — Arthur was, first and foremost, a fierce battle leader — Nennius is quite clear that Arthur's victories were dedicated to God. Third, the feats ascribed to Arthur have made him larger than life; that is the least we can say of a man credited with killing 960 of the enemy on a single day.

The next historical report of Arthur's deeds, the *Annals of Wales*, was written around 950. Like the other historical accounts, it was written in Latin and was the work of an unknown Welsh monk. Arthur is referred to twice. Under the accounts for the year 517 we learn that Arthur's shield bore "the Cross of our Lord Jesus Christ," and that he was victorious at the Battle of Badon, which lasted three days and three nights. There is more information for the year 538, in which we learn of "the Battle of Camlann, where Arthur and Medraut [Mordred] fell." This is the first reference to one of the several figures who will be associated with Arthur. Although Mordred appears here as a warrior who fought, apparently on Arthur's side, and died, later he will be transformed into Arthur's nephew (sometimes his son) and become a treacherous villain. As for the whereabouts of Camlann, it is as unknown as Badon, or any of the 12 battle sites mentioned by Nennius.

Numerous other Welsh sources help us shape our picture of Arthur. One is a kind of writing, a mixture of fact and legend, called saints' lives. These are biographies of important religious figures, often those who founded monasteries. The author of a saint's life, normally a fellow monk, living in the monastery that the saint had founded, sought to glorify the founder and to develop a reverence for objects associated with him. The goal was to increase religious devotion, not to strive for accuracy of character or event. One of the usual features of these writings — saints' lives tended to be very much like one another — is the conversion of a ruffian, and Arthur is one of the frequent objects of such conversion. When first seen in these lives he is a lout and a bully; by the end he has been reformed, and is submissive to the saint of the story. The whole point is to celebrate the power of the

> *Arthur, once and future king, remains the object of furious controversy. A native Celtic king? A pure fiction with or without a basis in reality? Perhaps an old Celtic god revived?*
> —WARD RUTHERFORD
> British historian

spiritual world over the secular world. To the monks who wrote these lives, Arthur's reputation as a fierce warrior probably made him an ideal candidate to demonstrate the saint's ability to reform character. Despite the fact that they are largely fictitious, the saints' lives offer two kinds of important clues to Arthur's identity. Sometimes they support other sources of information about Arthur, for example, that he was a warrior who relied upon cavalry, and

The Saxon invasion provided the cause for the rise of a leader such as Arthur. At the Battle of Badon in the beginning of the 6th century, Arthur, although not a king, is thought to have commanded the British forces to victory against the invaders.

that he was a Briton. Sometimes they add new details; some of the familiar persons associated with Arthur — Kay, Bedevere, and Guinevere — are introduced in these legends.

The gaps that appear in Gildas's text, the exaggerations that adorn Nennius's work, and the fantasy element that has crept into the saints' lives make it easy to see why some historians still refuse to believe in the existence of Arthur.

3

A King in Transition

History and story — they are enjoyed for different reasons, and different standards are demanded of the two. In earlier times, however, the distinction between history and story was less important. Frequently, the Arthur of history and the Arthur of story existed comfortably in the same piece of writing; later the Arthur of story completely submerged the Arthur of history. But even in the earliest histories, Arthur's feats were legendary. From the very first reference to Arthur, in the *Gododdin*, to later Welsh poems that provided him with a court and followers, the legend of Arthur grew, rooted in fact, certainly, but also embellished with the magic and grandeur that have made his name live on far longer than might have been expected for a mere border chieftain living far from the centers of civilization.

Examples of the British leader's legendary powers are common even in the earliest writings. In Nennius's account of Arthur the summary of the 12 battles is followed by two miraculous events. The first concerns a heap of stones, the top of which contained the footprint of Arthur's dog, Cabal. According to the story, no matter how far from the pile the stone was taken, the next day it would be found back at the top of that pile. The second miraculous event concerns Arthur's son, Anir, who had been

> *From the very roots of Arthurian romance . . . the borderline between the romantic dreamworld and the military reality was always indistinct.*
> —RICHARD BARBER
> British historian

Stained glass window depicting King Arthur astride a camel. The legend of the warrior king spread well beyond the borders of Britain, even as far as the Middle East. Arthur thus was sometimes portrayed mounted on animals not normally found in western Europe.

While in the company of kings, Arthur takes another knight into his service. As the story of Arthur began to supersede the actual history of Arthur, tales of other knights and kings began to be woven into his tale.

killed and then buried by Arthur. Nennius tells us that when the length of the mound was measured, sometimes it was found to be six feet, sometimes nine, sometimes twelve, and sometimes fifteen. "I myself proved this to be true," said Nennius. Arthur is no longer a mere warrior; through Nennius he has become a defender of his people, a follower of Christ, and a magnet for lesser miracles.

Welsh secular poetry also contributes to the changing portrait of the Arthur of history. In one poem, dating from the 10th or 11th century, Arthur is associated with Celtic gods. Because Wales was at the edge of Roman Britain, Christianity had never totally eradicated the old pagan beliefs of the people. In this poem Arthur and his men raid the island stronghold of the gods and carry off as plunder a magical cooking vessel, a cauldron that would not boil meat for a coward.

A more complete story is the tale of "Kulhwch and Olwen." The earliest version dates from the 11th century, but as these songs were sung and recited long before they were written down, the story is certainly much older, for the presence of Arthur in the story is somewhat incidental; he is not the central figure of the legend. The story relates the adventures of the warrior Kulhwch, who has to perform a series of 12 labors to win the hand in marriage of Olwen, a giant's daughter. Kulhwch comes to Arthur's court to ask for aid. In the course of his adventures, which eventually end in the winning of Olwen's hand, more than 200 members of Arthur's court are presented. Kay and Bedevere appear again, and, in the course of the story, Kay and Arthur quarrel and we are told that Kay would not help Arthur in his final hour of need. Gawain is noted among Arthur's men for the first time. The story also repeats the motif, or recurring theme, of the magic cauldron and its nine guardian maidens. In these secular tales, magic and myth are featured more prominently than are the history and Christianity that predominate in the earlier, more historical accounts of King Arthur.

Because in these tales the Arthur of history is being replaced by the Arthur of story, it is appro-

Sir Gawain waits on a magical bed in a German manuscript illustration of the tale *Sir Gawain and the Green Knight*. This tale of knightly virtue and honor was not directly incorporated into the Arthurian saga, but rather the main character was utilized for other, similar stories within the Arthurian legend.

This 16th-century French tapestry depicting ladies of Arthur's court cavorting with unicorns and lions clearly shows the change in orientation of the Arthurian legend from war to romance and fantasy.

46

priate to stop now and summarize our knowledge of the Arthur of history. Drawing upon all sources, archeological, historical, and literary, two biographical sketches may be drawn. The first portrait infers much from the scant records in order to establish a rather complete career. The second is a more conservative statement, allowing only for what is indisputable fact.

In the first version, Arthur is born about 475 to a Welsh family and grows up strongly influenced by Roman institutions. As a young man, he allies himself with Ambrosius, king of the Britons, who is looking for a successor. Arthur develops skill in cavalry warfare, and he conducts military campaigns in defense of Christianity, while associating himself with the Blessed Virgin Mary. He succeeds Ambrosius, and wages several fierce and successful campaigns in the west and north against the advancing Saxon invaders. His final battle at Badon in 517 is his greatest victory; the Saxons are driven back and 40 years of relative peace follow. Arthur then dies at the Battle of Camlann along with Mordred in 538.

The second version has Arthur simply as a British warrior of the early 6th century who distinguished himself in battle against the Saxon invaders.

Thus, though only part of the full biography seems to be verifiable, all of it may actually be true. Historians disagree about the details, though most no longer doubt, as earlier historians had doubted, that there was a historical Arthur, renowned as a leader against the Saxons in the 6th century.

It is sure, however, that Arthur's triumph and the subsequent peace were short-lived. By 600 the Saxons had subdued nearly all of Britain except for the three lands of Cornwall, Wales, and Scotland. Many Britons also fled to the continent of Europe and settled in the northwestern arm of France, from that time on known as Brittany. It might be expected that the reputation of Arthur, the leader whose victories merely provided a little time of peace for the British, would have vanished in obscurity. After all, it is the victors who write the histories. But Arthur's fame did not end. Why did the legend of Arthur continue to grow?

As time passed and the legends of Arthur grew, historical fact was submerged. The more historical image of the Arthurian knight as a 6th-century British warrior dressed in chain mail and carrying a broadsword and spear gave way to the more romantic, lance-wielding knight adorned in a full suit of plate mail riding his trusty war-horse.

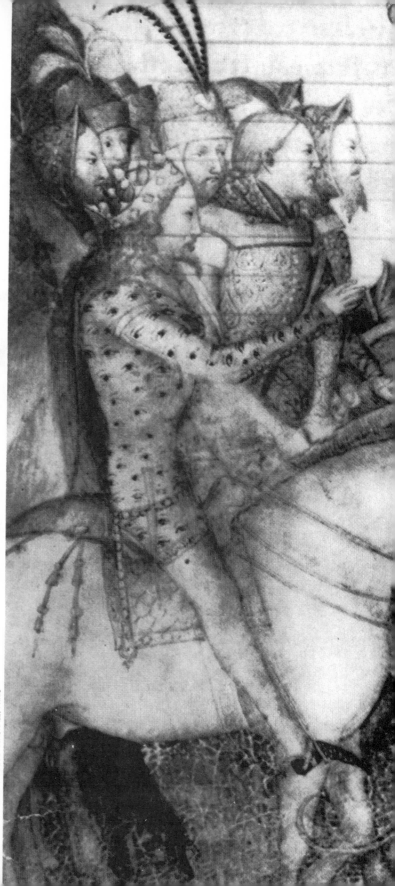

Arthur (left), his dog, Cabal, and his knights ride off on an adventure as Sir Gawain (center), with sword raised high, wards off an approaching rider.

4

The Legend in Norman England

The Norman conquest of England in 1066 marks one of the most momentous changes in English history. It was then that the Normans, Scandinavians who had settled long before in what is now the French province of Normandy, led by William the Conqueror, defeated the English King Harold at the much celebrated Battle of Hastings.

The Normans made vast cultural and administrative changes in England. As conquerors, they made French the official language of the nobility and courts. Feudalism superseded the old Anglo-Saxon system of government, which was based on the loyalty of warriors to their *thegns*, or lords. All power in feudal societies rested officially with the king, and through him it was distributed to nobles, who governed lesser nobles. At the bottom of the social order were the peasants, or serfs, who were obliged to work for their lords in exchange for food, protection, and justice. Stone castles, long used in continental Europe to control the areas around them, began to dominate the English countryside.

Into this changing land rode the Arthur of story.

The court of Arthur was made the center of many cycles of courtly romances—of tales of knightly prowess performed to do honor to ladies.
—CHRISTOPHER BROOKE
British historian, on the Arthurian myth in the Middle Ages

A romantic vision of Arthur and Guinevere embracing each other on horseback outside of the magnificent castle Camelot. Such picturesque scenes of idyllic love were often the central theme for many of the tales of Arthur.

In 1066 the superior forces of William the Conqueror of Normandy defeated the English troops of King Harold at the Battle of Hastings. The new Norman rulers imposed the French language and culture upon Britain.

> *[Arthur] is the fount of all honor, his court the magnet to which all knights are drawn.*
> —RICHARD BARBER
> British historian

In 1137 Geoffrey of Monmouth, who is believed to have been a member of a Norman family that had taken part in the invasion of England and then settled in Wales, collected the scattered stories of Arthur and compiled them in a single work. Geoffrey's book, *The History of the Kings of Britain*, was an enormously popular and influential work in its own day and for centuries after. It is most responsible for transmitting the fame of Arthur beyond the Welsh borders. The *History* is dedicated to the earl of Gloucester, one of the Norman lords who had gained power in Britain after the conquest. At the time that Geoffrey wrote, authors were not, like the Welsh monks, hoping to gain God's favor, or, like modern authors, seeking public sales of their books, but rather were trying to gain the support of a powerful noble patron.

But why might Geoffrey have believed that a Norman lord such as the earl of Gloucester would be favorably impressed by a history of an ancient line of British rulers?

Some historians believe that the Norman ruling class sought a hero to match the popular French hero and king, Charlemagne. Another explanation is that Geoffrey perhaps thought that his story of the 99 kings of Britain might supply the Norman rulers with a tradition to follow, allowing them to believe that they had assumed control of a nation with a most worthy and ancient heritage. Indeed, there could be no greater heritage than the one Geoffrey claimed for the British. In Geoffrey's time the political system of the Roman Republic was regarded as the most perfect one ever developed, and, according to his *History*, the British, through their first king, Brutus, were directly connected to the greatness of Rome. Furthermore, one of their last rulers, King Arthur, had almost conquered the decadent remains of the Roman Empire. It would be indeed flattering for the Normans to believe that they had conquered a people with such great and noble traditions.

The History of the Kings of Britain asks the reader to believe a great deal indeed. First of all, Geoffrey discloses he did not write the book at all, but merely

King Arthur in a stained glass window from 15th-century Germany. As the British king remained a hero over the centuries in various countries, he acquired a wide variety of costumes. Here he stands in late medieval armor bearing a shield adorned with the eagle emblem often used by the German nobility.

translated into Latin "a certain most ancient book in the British language," written by Walter, archdeacon of Oxford. Of course, there was no written "British language" to be translated from, and no one now believes that there was any Walter, archdeacon of Oxford. The first king in Geoffrey's list is Brutus, grandson of Aeneas, the legendary founder of Rome in the poet Virgil's epic Latin work, the *Aeneid*.

Geoffrey is merely following Virgil's example in creating characters with distinguished ancestries when no written records exist about the people of earlier eras. Virgil's Aeneas is fictitious; so is Geoffrey's Brutus; so, for that matter, are most of the 99 kings of Britain whose reigns Geoffrey describes. His book might accurately be called a hoax, but such an accusation makes little sense when applied in

A section of the Bayeux Tapestry, an 11th-century embroidery that tells the story of the Norman Conquest. This particular section of the tapestry depicts the coming of Halley's comet and the eventual downfall of the English King Harold.

an age in which the distinction between history and fiction was of little importance. Certainly, however slight the value of Geoffrey's *History* as history, its value in spreading the story and the fame of Arthur is incalculable.

Arthur, the 91st king in Geoffrey's chronicle, did not exist in the way Geoffrey describes him. In the *History*, Arthur is by far the most important of the British kings; nearly one-quarter of the book is devoted to his reign. The sources for Geoffrey's life of Arthur were varied — the early histories of Gildas and Nennius; Welsh, British, and continental European legend and folklore; as well as Geoffrey's own

The imperial coronation in 800 of Charles the Great, or Charlemagne, king of the Franks and ruler of the Holy Roman Empire. The lasting prestige of Charlemagne was so overwhelming that some historians believe that the Normans in England embellished the legend of King Arthur in order to have a hero equal to the Frankish ruler.

imagination. But the nature of Geoffrey's account of Arthur's life owes less to sources than to Geoffrey's own literary talents. It is the first account of King Arthur that can claim completeness and that can be read with sustained interest. An excellent story, its popularity is not surprising.

Geoffrey was the first to present an account of Arthur's birth, though whether it is his own story or whether from a legend that he knew we cannot be certain. According to Geoffrey, these were the circumstances: the 90th British king, Uther Pendragon, after seeing Ygerne [Igraine], the young, beautiful wife of Gorlios, the duke of Cornwall, at

an Easter festival becomes passionately desirous of her. " 'I am desperately in love with Ygerne,' says Uther, 'and if I cannot have her I am convinced that I shall suffer a physical breakdown.' "

To help Uther overcome his pain, Geoffrey introduces a new character to the story of Arthur — the wizard Merlin. The origin of Merlin can be traced back to the Welsh bard and prophet Myrddin, who was well known in the West Country during the reigns of Ambrosius and Vortigern. Geoffrey makes the character more dramatic by giving him magical powers, which in turn supplies the fantastic element to the Arthurian story that becomes predominant later.

Enlisting the aid of the wizard Merlin, Uther is transformed into the likeness of the duke. Igraine, completely taken in by this deception, and thinking Uther to be her husband, sleeps with him. "That night she conceived Arthur, the most famous of men, who subsequently won great renown by his outstanding bravery."

After Igraine's husband dies in battle, Uther marries her, thus legitimizing Arthur. Upon the king's death, Arthur, now 15, succeeds to the throne of Britain. He immediately goes forth in battle and wins a series of campaigns against the Saxons, Picts, Scots, and Irish. Here Geoffrey followed Nennius, though he reduced the number of battles from twelve to three and gave them identifiable locations. For example, the Battle of Badon was placed in the city of Bath, in western England.

Describing the young king at the battle, Geoffrey states: "Arthur himself put on a leather jerkin worthy of so great a king. On his head he placed a golden helmet, with a crest carved in the shape of a dragon; and across his shoulders a circular shield called Pridwen, on which there was painted a likeness of the Blessed Mary, Mother of God, which forced him to be thinking perpetually of her. He girded on his peerless sword, called Caliburn, which was forged in the Isle of Avalon. A spear called Ron graced his right hand: long, broad in the blade and thirsty for slaughter."

Later during the Battle of Badon, after many unsuccessful attacks, Arthur "drew his sword Caliburn, called upon the name of the Blessed Virgin, and rushed forward at full speed into the thickest ranks of the enemy. Every man whom he struck,

A mosaic of the Roman poet Virgil and two muses. Virgil's famous work, the *Aeneid*, describes a fictitious history of the foundation of Rome by the Trojan hero Aeneas. In the same way that Virgil painted Rome's past with glory, Geoffrey of Monmouth in *The History of the Kings of Britain* ennobled Britain's past by having Aeneas's grandson become the first king of Britain.

The wizard Merlin approaches Nimue, the Lady of the Lake. Fantastic powers were attributed to Merlin, who was said to be the offspring of a human female and an incubus (male demon). The late tales of Arthur describe Merlin as the king's closest confidant and one of his most powerful allies.

calling upon God as he did so, he killed at a single blow. He did not slacken in his onslaught until he dispatched four hundred and seventy men with his sword Caliburn. . . . The Saxons, who only a short time before used to attack like lightning in the most ferocious way imaginable, now ran away with fear in their hearts."

Arthur then marries Ganhumara, later known as Guinevere, a noble woman of a Roman family, who "did surpass in beauty all of the other dames of the island." Following 12 years of peace, during which Arthur holds his court at "the City of Legions" on the Usk River, he subdues Norway, Denmark, and Gaul (the Roman name for present-day France). There is no known source for Geoffrey's account of these adventures. Many of them probably derive from tales that had become associated with Arthur, for others we must credit Geoffrey's imagination.

Arthur returns to Britain to be crowned king, but even before the lavish coronation festival is concluded, he receives a demand from the Roman Emperor Lucius for tribute payments. Arthur decides not to pay, for he believes that because the Romans had taken the Britons' rightful land centuries before, the emperor should be paying tribute to him. To achieve this goal Arthur sails to the continent, where his ambassador, Gawain, defies the emperor and fights him bravely. However, just as Arthur is about to enter Rome, news arrives at the British camp that his nephew, Mordred, "in whose care he had left Britain, had placed the crown upon his own head. What is more, this treacherous tyrant was living adulterously and out of wedlock with Queen Guinevere, who had broken the vows of her earlier marriage."

Arthur returns to Britain with Gawain, who is slain when they land, and pursues Mordred's forces into Cornwall, the most southwestern region of England. During a mighty battle Mordred is slain, and "Arthur himself our renowned King, was wounded deadly and was carried off to the Isle of Avalon, so that his wounds might be attended to." These climactic events — Mordred's treachery, Guinevere's forced marriage, Arthur's pursuit of Mordred into

> *In the world of marvels which lies outside the gates of Arthur's court, the knights are the dispensers of justice in an evil and hostile world.*
> —RICHARD BARBER
> British historian

Cornwall, and the final battle — are taken from the tradition that had grown up about the Battle of Camlann, first recorded in the *Annals of Wales*. The departure for Avalon is the last we hear of Arthur in Geoffrey's *History*. The year is 542, and Geoffrey reports that the throne passes to the 92nd king, Arthur's kinsman, Constantine.

King Arthur (left center; wearing crowned helm) and his knights charge enemy forces under the dragon standard. The use of this banner signified Arthur's descent from Uther Pendragon.

King Arthur, dressed in a long surcoat of chain mail and crowned dragon helm, kisses Guinevere before joining his comrades-in-arms. Romantic relationships between chivalrous lords and their ladies became prevalent as the legend of Arthur grew.

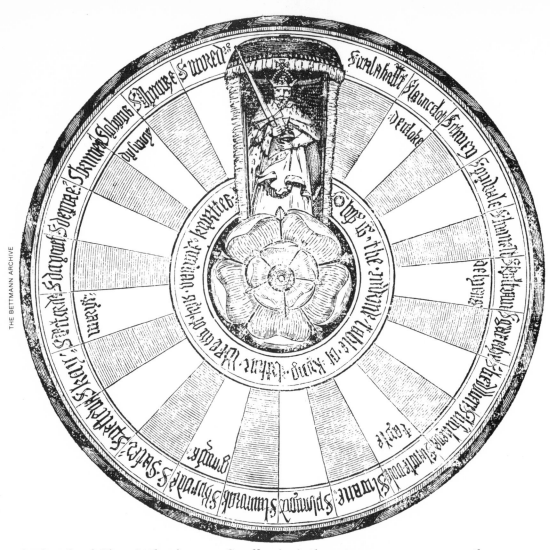

A sketch of King Arthur's Round Table. The concept of the Round Table — a shape allowing all of the knights to have an equal status — was introduced into the legend by the Norman poet Wace. This particular table was constructed in the late 15th century for Henry VII of England (note the rose in the center, the symbol of the Tudor line of royalty) and may still be seen today in Winchester Castle.

Geoffrey's Arthur is more superman than man. He is victorious in battle despite being seriously outnumbered. With the aid of his sword, Caliburn, he twice defeats giants. It is mostly as a warrior that we see him. His fierce battles are fought in the name of Britain and Christ. The conquest of the Scots and Picts is typically gruesome. He puts them to rout, and they take refuge on an island in Loch (Lake) Lomond.

> Although they gained little help from it. Arthur collected together a fleet of boats and sailed round the rivers. By besieging his enemies for fifteen days he reduced them to such a state of famine that they died in their thousands. . . . He treated them with unparalleled

severity, sparing no one who fell into his hands. As a result all the bishops of this pitiful country, with all the clergy under their command, their feet bare and in their relics of their saints and their treasures of their churches, assembled to beg the King for the relief of their people.

Arthur finally relents, but Arthur the ruler is much less important in Geoffrey's work than Arthur the warrior. Except for one long description of Arthur's coronation, which historians believe must have been based upon Geoffrey's observations of court ceremonies in his own time, court life and feudal organization receive little treatment. The Arthur of Geoffrey of Monmouth is primarily what he always had been, in history and in story, a fabulous fighter for God and country.

Geoffrey of Monmouth's *History of the Kings of Britain*, which was written in Latin, had a great influence on its times. It was soon followed by French and English translations. By means of these translations into the common tongue, the story of Arthur could be read by persons who knew only their native language, particularly women, very few of whom could read Latin. In addition, these translations added to the growing reputation of Arthur. The translation into French by the Norman poet Wace describes the Round Table, around which Arthur's knights met. Because there was no head of the table, no one at the Round Table could claim superiority. And it is Wace who adds the legend that someday Arthur will return from his convalescence in Avalon to rule Britain again.

Wace, in turn, was translated into English by Layamon, a priest, who nearly doubled the length of the text. Like everyone else who had written or who would write about Arthur, Layamon too adds details found nowhere else. To the legend of Arthur's final battle wound, for example, Layamon adds the fairies who bear the dead king away in a magic boat to dwell with his elder half-sister, Morgan le Fay. She will use her magical arts to make Arthur's wound whole, so that one day he may return to rule his kingdom.

69

After the Battle of Camlann the mortally wounded Arthur is taken on a barge to the magical isle of Avalon. The faerie ladies surrounding the king may be attributed to the imagination of the English priest Layamon.

5

Tales from Abroad

The Arthurian legend spread beyond England and throughout Europe, where it rivaled the greatest stories of the period. The common people heard it sung by bards; at court, poets wrote their own versions. In each retelling, the speaker — by careful selection of details, by appropriate emphasis, and by introduction of new elements — adapted the story to the particular needs of the time and the audience. In the late 12th century, a French poet, Chrétien de Troyes, wrote five tales concerning King Arthur's court: *Eric et Enide*, *Cliges*, *Yvain*, *Perceval*, and *Lancelot*. Perhaps taking a hint from Geoffrey's brief account of the 12-year interval of peace between the Saxon and Roman wars, Chrétien introduces Camelot, the court of Arthur, as the gathering place of noble and courageous lords and of beautiful and chaste ladies. It was a place of banquets and tournaments, in short, the finest court that ever has been. In Chrétien de Troyes's tales, the deeds of King Arthur are less important than the society of his court and the tales of the knights and ladies who assemble there.

Like Geoffrey of Monmouth, who created an Arthur who would be suitable to the Norman society

The stories of Arthur and his court were common ground for Spanish, Italian, Portuguese, French, German and English knights, and there are even pieces in Hebrew, Greek, Latin and Norse.
—RICHARD BARBER
British historian

Tristan and Isolt, a tale of a tragic love affair, was incorporated into the Arthurian legend. Here Tristan brings the Irish Princess Isolt to Cornwall to marry his uncle, King Mark. Tristan and Isolt partake in a love potion that causes a forbidden love affair — a typical theme in tales of courtly love.

for which he wrote, Chrétien adapted the Arthurian stories so that they embodied ideas and feelings that were particularly pertinent to the France of his own time. In Chrétien's stories, the rugged, masculine world featured in earlier tales of Arthur and his knights has been largely replaced by a study of the tensions arising from different codes of love and honor, and the opposing demands of worldly life and spiritual life.

One of Chrétien's tales concerns the Holy Grail, the cup reputedly used by Jesus at the Last Supper, and also said to maintain drops of Jesus's blood. According to legend, the cup was retrieved and brought to England by Joseph of Arimathea, the figure in the New Testament who took Jesus's body from the cross and laid it in the tomb.

In Chrétien's tale *Perceval* the young knight reaches a castle surrounded by wasteland, and is greeted by the keeper of the castle, an old, lame man fishing in a river. Inside the castle, Perceval sees the Grail. He asks no questions. The next morning he wakes to find the castle deserted. Later, a young girl tells him that his host was the Fisher King, who had been made lame by a wound. She adds that if Perceval had asked about the Grail, the wounds would have been healed and the land about the castle renewed. Five years pass. Perceval learns from a hermit, who proves to be his uncle, that the Fisher King is also his uncle, and that their father, Perceval's grandfather, has been kept alive by a communion host borne in the Holy Grail.

Chrétien's story is a confusing one, for the motivations of the characters are unclear. An explanation has been offered for this confusion. According to this explanation, the Grail story is a Christian retelling of an old pagan story concerning heroes and their quests for mystical chalices, much like the early Celtic story of Arthur and the magical cooking vessel. The story that underlies the Grail legend is about fertility, how human life is produced from death in the annual miracle of spring succeeding winter. With the addition of the Grail it became a story about Christianity: how eternal life is produced from death through the sacrifice of

Christ on the Cross.

Chrétien's most common subject, however, is the problems arising from earthly love. Perhaps his most famous story in this regard deals with the ro-

King Arthur and the knights of the Round Table receive a vision of the Holy Grail in this 15th-century French book illustration. The search for the Grail, the chalice that contained the blood of Christ, was one of the most consistent and lengthy tales from the late medieval versions of King Arthur.

mance of Lancelot (Launcelot) and Guinevere. Chrétien and other poets of his time were influenced by a code called "courtly love." This part of the chivalric code of knights may be summarized as follows: knights, in addition to possessing the military vir-

Sir Galahad, tired and dispirited from his seemingly endless search for the Holy Grail, receives a welcome visitation from three guiding angels. Only three knights have ever been noted for completing the near impossible quest: Sir Galahad, Sir Bors, and Sir Perceval.

tue of courage, were expected to excel in a wide range of other human virtues, including piety, generosity, and especially courtesy. According to Chrétien, the gallant French knight Sir Lancelot was the epitome of all these traits.

A German manuscript illustration depicts Sir Perceval standing ready to begin his quest for the Holy Grail, while a squire holds his warhorse steady. The story of Sir Perceval was a favorite among the Germans. In 1882 composer Richard Wagner based his last opera, *Parsifal*, on the knight's story.

Included in the virtue of courtesy was courtly love. ("Courtesy" derives from "court.") In a time in which marriage among the nobility was a contract entered into to fulfill social and political obligations rather than being a sanctification of mutual love, courtly love spoke to the reality of romantic, passionate attachment between men and women. According to its code of conduct, the courtly lover (in this case, Lancelot) worships a beautiful lady (Arthur's queen, Guinevere), his love known to all but her. To prove the sincerity of his love, he undertakes whatever she commands, without question or hesitation, willing to risk everything to please her. (Lancelot, in fact,

Queen Guinevere dubs Sir Launcelot her champion. As
the queen's sworn protector, Launcelot would battle any
foe for the safety or honor of his lady. The knight and
queen were, however, to go one step further and begin
an illicit love affair that eventually caused the destruction of the fellowship of the Round Table.

risks the destruction of the Round Table.) Two principles follow from this type of relationship. First, since courtly love is freely given, it cannot exist between husband and wife, for their marriage was not voluntary. Second, since courtly love is often sexual, the doctrines of courtly love conclude that adultery

Although a priest sits between them, Queen Guinevere and Sir Launcelot exchange a kiss. The love affair between the queen and knight was introduced into the legend of Arthur in the 12th century by the French poet Chrétien de Troyes.

is somewhat permissible. It is thus easy to understand that the incompatibility of courtly love with Christian ethics was a major problem in Arthurian literature.

Another favorite love story of the Middle Ages, the love of Tristan and Isolt, is not told by Chrétien de Troyes. Its finest telling of the period is by the German writer Gottfried of Strasbourg, who wrote around 1210. Like all of the stories that became associated with Arthur's court, the story of Tristan was doubtless told and sung by bards before it was written down. It is the story of the love triangle of King Mark of Cornwall, his nephew Tristan, and princess Isolt of Ireland. Tristan wins the favor of King Mark by killing the Irish warrior Morolt, in a combat in which he himself suffers a grave poison sword wound. In the course of his recovery he goes to Ireland and meets Isolt. He is unaware that she is Morolt's niece, and she does not know that he is her uncle's killer. After Tristan returns to Cornwall, Mark is urged to marry Isolt, and Tristan is sent to bring the king's bride to him. However, during the course of their return to Cornwall, the two accidentally drink a love potion. For four years of intrigue, discovery, and disgrace they are adulterous lovers. In exile, Tristan suffers a second poison wound from an enemy's tainted spear; this time Isolt does not arrive in time to save him, and she takes her own life. As a wound had earlier united them in love, a wound now unites them in death. Gottfried's telling of this story of courtly love raises social questions about forced marriage and about individual needs. It is noteworthy that this passionate, romantic conception of love, which arose in the Middle Ages and is thought to have been invented by poets, has remained, and is a part of our own views on love.

In these stories of the Grail and of Tristan and Isolt, King Arthur is in the background. But he is not, because of that, unimportant. Writers of the Middle Ages believed that Arthur was a person of historical significance — an unparalleled warrior and noble Christian. These assumptions were widely accepted by medieval readers. The stories about the lords and ladies of Arthur's court gain impact and dignity from his presence, even when he is only a minor figure. That the Arthur of history has been completely replaced by the Arthur of story is much clearer to us from our own vantage point of several centuries distance than it was to persons living in the Middle Ages.

The romance of Tristan and Isolt is an ill-fated one, for Isolt is the wife of Tristan's uncle. Unable to deal with the grief of being near his lady and yet forbidden to love her, Tristan leaves Cornwall to travel abroad.

6

The Death of Arthur

It is characteristic of legendary heroes such as King Arthur to draw into their orbit previously unrelated tales and motifs. This process can be seen at work from the earliest origins of the story of Arthur. Nennius provided him with a dog and a son. In "Kulhwch and Olwen," Arthur's court was the center for the adventures of other heroes. Later, even the Tristan and Isolt and the Grail legends attached themselves to Arthur's court.

Significant differences have been noted between the Arthur of history and the figure who supplanted him during the course of the Middle Ages, the Arthur of story. The Arthur of history is always the strong central figure. The Arthur of story is most often a secondary figure; it is the adventures of his knights — Launcelot, Gawain, Gareth, Tristram (Tristan) and the others — that hold our attention. But even as King Arthur's active role diminishes in these tales, his role as a model of chivalric virtues and as a character vulnerable to the actions of others increases. The Arthur of story is altogether human, and a far more complicated and interesting character than the Arthur of history.

The literature in which the ideal of knighthood was set forth had probably little influence on the art of government or the practical life of society at large; its impact was on the individual in his social conduct, in the refinement of his emotions and manners.
—R. W. SOUTHERN
American historian

A stained glass rendition of King Arthur the warrior — complete with a full suit of plate armor, a white horse, and his shield of the holy mother and child. By the late Middle Ages, the legend of King Arthur had evolved in such a manner that the king no longer did much fighting but rather dispatched knights to battle when necessary.

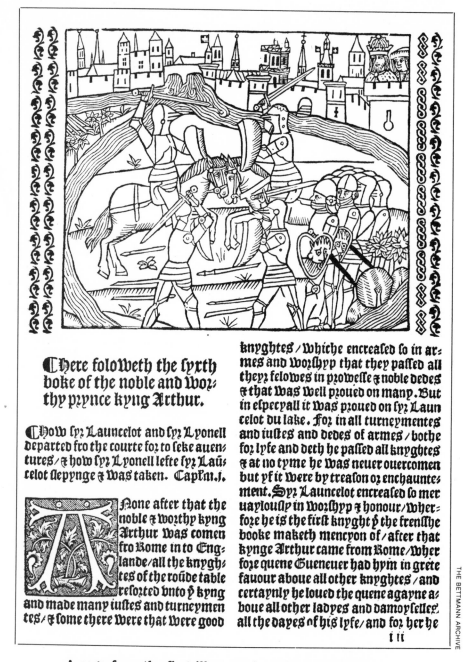

A page from the first illustrated version of Sir Thomas Malory's *Morte d'Arthur*, printed in 1529. The first version of the book was printed in 1485 by William Caxton, who wished to make available to all readers the valuable lessons from Arthur's age of honor and chivalry.

Nonetheless, these later authors and troubadours who wrote and sang of Arthur and his court fully believed that they were writing about a person who once lived and ruled. That is probably the reason why, despite differences in interpretation and emphasis from one telling to the next, there remains a central, unchanging core to his character. Consequently, it is possible to describe in general terms the character of Arthur as it was presented to audiences of the Middle Ages.

What is he like? He is less a warrior than is the Arthur of history; it is his knights who mostly do battle, proving their loyalty to him by undertaking the challenges that arise. He is an open-hearted and generous person, but sometimes suffers from the excess of this virtue, for he has a tendency to have favorites, some of whom, Launcelot particularly, prove to be unworthy of his trust. He is forgiving of others, and never goes back on his word. He is a pious and valiant Christian, though not an intensely spiritual man. Unlike his knights Perceval, Galahad, and Bors, Arthur never achieves an understanding of the Holy Grail or an intense spiritual love of God.

Perhaps the greatest of all stories of Arthur comes toward the end of the Middle Ages. It was written around 1470 by Sir Thomas Malory, and printed as *Morte d'Arthur* (*The Death of Arthur*) in 1485 by the first English printer, William Caxton. The invention of movable type, which made printing possible, allowed books to be produced mechanically in great numbers. This development played a role in the history of King Arthur that cannot be ignored. Previously, every copy of a book had to be written by hand. The more books, of course, the more readers, and as it is less expensive to print than to copy a book, printing allows the possibility of a mass audience. One other consequence of printing, though less obvious, is no less profound. Printed books signaled the end of oral transmission of literature, the means whereby the stories of Arthur had gradually developed and were embellished, and thus could almost be said to be the product of a whole culture more than of a single author. After the invention of

[Arthur] is in many ways the knight's ideal monarch: generous, eager for the renown of his knights, concerned that there shall be adventures for them to undertake.
—RICHARD BARBER
British historian

the printing press individual writers such as Malory were better able to present their own unique version of Arthur, written for their own prestige.

Information about Malory is scarce. It is known that he lived in the 15th century during the bloody English civil war period known as the Wars of the Roses. Malory spent much of his life in prison, where he was sentenced for a number of charges, mostly political, and where he was often detained while awaiting trial. It is thought that he must have had access to a good prison library, for his book about King Arthur is based on a large number of English and French sources. As a matter of fact, in his preface to Malory's work, Caxton argues that Malory's purpose in writing about Arthur was primarily a moral one. He complains that Arthur was better known among other peoples — the Dutch, Italians, Germans, Greeks, and French — than he was among the English people. Consistent with the opinions of his time, Caxton states that, although not everything written about Arthur may be true, his historical existence cannot be doubted. It was not the truth of Arthur's story, however, that led Caxton to print the book, but its morality.

Caxton realized that Malory was writing about a time far distant than the one he was living in. Caxton believed that the tales of King Arthur would be useful for his divided countrymen because they could remind the English of the grandeur their land once had. The Arthurian stories could teach "the noble acts of chivalry, the loyal and virtuous deeds by which some knights in those days came to honor and how they that were vicious were punished and often put to shame and rebuke." By reading the stories of Arthur, Caxton hoped that everyone, "noble lords and ladies and all other estates, no matter what their estate or degree, that shall see and read in this said book and work, . . . take the good and honest acts in their remembrance and follow the same, wherein they shall find many joyous and pleasant histories and noble and renowned acts of humanity, gentleness, and chivalry. For herein may be seen noble chivalry, courtesy, humanity, friendliness, hardiness, love, friendship, cowardice, mur-

THE ROMANCE OF KING ARTHUR AND THE KNIGHTS OF THE ROUND TABLE, ABRIDGED A. W. POLLARD, MACMILLAN

Igraine gives the baby Arthur to Merlin. The wizard and
King Uther had agreed that if Merlin supplied the magic
allowing Uther to seduce Igraine, the wife of his enemy
Duke Gorlios, the child conceived that night would be
delivered to Merlin to be raised away from the court.

der, hate, virtue, and sin. Go after the good and leave the evil, and it shall bring you good fame and renown."

Caxton channeled the myriad legends set down by Malory into a framework unified by the career of King Arthur. *Morte d'Arthur* opens and closes with stories of the king. The first portion of the book describes Arthur's birth as well as his political and military career, culminating in his victory over the Roman Emperor Lucius. The ending describes the breakdown of the Round Table, the fateful Battle of Camlann, and the departure of Arthur to Avalon. The first inner layer concerns Launcelot, recounting his spectacular arrival at King Arthur's court, and later the sad story of his adulterous relationship with Queen Guenevere (Guinevere), by which he betrayed his king. The other tales in the work are stories that had come to be associated with King Arthur's court. Among these are "The Tale of Sir Garth of Orkney," which uses Camelot as the starting place for a series of adventures exemplifying the chivalric code; the romantic story of Tristram (Tristan) and Isolde (Isolt); as well as the quest for the Holy Grail. However, according to Malory it is Launcelot's son, Galahad, and Sir Bors, as well as Chrétien de Troyes's Perceval, who find the holy vessel.

In comparison to his predecessors, Malory is considered a realistic writer. That is, whenever possible he tries to provide natural rather than supernatural explanations of events. Nonetheless, Malory continues the direction Arthur had taken, that is, from history to story. Malory's Arthur is pure myth. A myth may be defined as a story that attempts to explain traditional beliefs through characters who possess supernatural powers and perform superhuman deeds. There are two ways of regarding myth. The first is to say that stories that contain impossible events, superhuman characters, and fantastic descriptions are simply unreal and untrue, and therefore useless. The second is to ask why myths survive so long after anyone believes them to be accounts of actual events, and why — almost because of their impossibility, unreality, and untruth — they continue to be useful.

As King Arthur approaches, the Lady of the Lake's arm, clothed in white samite, rises out of the water holding aloft the sword Excalibur. As long as the king wore the enchanted sword's scabbard he would lose no blood.

A late 19th-century tapestry depicting chain-mail-clad knights being led by an angel while on the quest for the Holy Grail. The quest is the principal theme linking the various knights' stories in Malory's *Morte d'Arthur*.

King Arthur (lower right) lies wounded, surrounded by the twisted remains of horses and knights after the Battle of Camlann. This 14th-century manuscript illustration colorfully conveys the carnage during the final clash between Arthur and his illegitimate son Mordred.

The features of Arthur's life correspond to the typical hero of myth. These include magical and mysterious circumstances of birth, a hidden heritage during childhood ending with sudden recognition of the hero's royalty, early struggles, complete success, and a climactic confrontation in which the hero dies and is celebrated in legend.

Malory's Arthur seems to follow this pattern perfectly. The hero's birth is mysterious, contrived by Merlin, the magician who brings Uther to Igraine in the guise of her husband, the duke of Cornwall, for a promise. " 'Sir,' said Merlin, 'this is my desire: the first night that ye shall lie by Igraine ye shall get a child on her, and when that is born, that it shall be delivered to me for to nourish there as I will have it.' "

Arthur is indeed born a few months later and is handed over to Merlin as promised; he in turn gives the boy to a local knight, Sir Ector, to raise as one of his own. When Uther dies, the realm stands in jeopardy, for every powerful lord desires the throne. Merlin arranges the sword in the stone test.

After Arthur successfully pulls the sword from the stone, many of the other knights rebel, but, through the assistance of Merlin's magic and through the power of his magic sword, which Malory names Excalibur, Arthur is victorious. Malory gives a second story of this enchanted weapon that indicates that Arthur's supreme knighthood is blessed by God. Following a battle in which the sword is broken and Arthur nearly killed, Merlin arranges for Arthur to receive another Excalibur: "So they rode till they came to a lake, the which was a fair water and broad, and in the midst of the lake Arthur was ware of an arm clothed in white samite, that held a fair sword in that hand. 'Lo!' said Merlin, 'Yonder is that sword I spake of.' " The king and the wizard row to the spot and Arthur takes the sword for his own. "Then Sir Arthur looked on the sword, and liked it passing well. 'Whether liketh you better,' said Merlin, 'the sword or the scabbard?' 'Me liketh better the sword,' said Arthur. 'Ye are much more unwise,' said Merlin, 'for the scabbard is worth ten of the swords, for whiles ye have the scabbard upon you, ye shall never

> *For I will into the vale of Avilion to heal me of my grievous wound; and if thou hear never more of me, pray for my soul.*
> —Arthur's last words, from Sir Thomas Malory's *Morte d'Arthur*

> *Don't let it be forgot*
> *That once there was a spot*
> *For one brief shining moment*
> *Known as Camelot.*
> —ALAN J. LERNER
> lyrics from the 20th-century
> play *Camelot*

lose no blood be ye ever so sore wounded, therefore keep well the scabbard always with you.' "

Arthur would not heed Merlin's advice this time, however, for he was so taken by the majesty of the sword that he cherished that most. Having already received this sword from the Lady of the Lake, and having already come into possession of the Round Table through his marriage to Guinevere, Arthur governed a society as perfect as could be imagined. The magical sword, Excalibur, guaranteed military invincibility and the Round Table ensured internal harmony.

For a time Arthur and his knights knew only success. Enemies were defeated, including the mightiest of all, the emperor of Rome. Following the account of Geoffrey of Monmouth, Malory has Arthur go to war against Lucius rather than pay the demanded tribute. The king travels to the continent, where, on his way to Rome, he kills the terrible giant of Michael's (or, in French, Michel's) Mount. In Rome he kills the Emperor Lucius himself.

Arthur then returns to Camelot, his court, which is renowned for its splendor, justice, and chivalry. Guinevere is the most beautiful of its women; the knights feel it an honor to carry out her bidding. But now, just at the high point of Arthur's career, the source of the destruction of his court enters. A newly arrived knight, Launcelot, achieves preeminence at court. "In all tournaments and jousts and deeds of arms, both for life and death, he passed all other knights, and at no time was overcome. . . . Queen Guenevere had him in great favour above all knights, and in certain he loved the queen again above all other ladies damosels of his life." However, his love for Guinevere, which was at first distant and worshipful, became adulterous.

During his quest for the Holy Grail, Launcelot vows to end this love, but upon his return his union with Guinevere becomes the scandal of the court, known to all but Arthur. When Arthur finally learns of their love he condemns Guinevere to die by being burned at the stake, and leaves to do battle with Launcelot, who has fled to France. In the battle Launcelot mortally wounds Sir Gawain, Arthur's

The weeping faerie queens comfort the wounded Arthur after the Battle of Camlann. In some versions, Arthur's stepsister Morgan le Fay is counted among their number.

Mordred lies dead (lower left), Excalibur is reclaimed by the Lady of the Lake (lower right), and Sir Bedevere (left) looks on as King Arthur sets sail for his resting place on the isle of Avalon.

most loyal and best-loved knight. Meanwhile, in his father's absence, Mordred seizes the throne, and makes it known that he will force Guinevere to marry him. Arthur returns, and a great battle between father and son ensues. At the final climax of the engagement:

> . . . the king gat his spear in both hands, and ran toward Mordred, crying, 'Traitor, now is thy death day come.'
>
> And when Sir Mordred heard Sir Arthur, he ran until him with his sword drawn in his hand. And there King Arthur smote Sir Mordred under the shield, with a foin [lunge] of his spear, throughout the body, more than a fathom. And when Sir Mordred felt that he had his death's wound he thrust himself with the might that he had up to the bur [handgrip] of King Arthur's spear. And right so he smote his father, Arthur, with his sword holden in both hands, on the side of the head, that the sword pierced the helmet and the brain pan, and therewithal Sir Mordred fell stark dead to the earth; and the noble Arthur fell in a swoon to the earth and there he swooned oft-times.

On Arthur's command, Excalibur is thrown in a lake where it is snatched by a woman's hand rising from the waves. In a barge Arthur leaves for Avalon, to be healed of his wounds. From there, it is said, he will return someday to save his people. When Guinevere learns of the departure of Arthur, she enters a convent and spends the rest of her life fasting, praying, and giving alms. She tells Launcelot, when he visits her, that they are responsible for the destruction of the Round Table. He sadly agrees with her judgment, and spends his declining years in prayer.

This is Malory's version of what is now called the myth of the hero. It touches our own lives and asks us to contemplate what is very important to us. As our own birth and death are shrouded in mystery from us, and as we imagine ourselves to be rare and special, and we also contemplate high hopes and great destinies, all the while fearing that these best plans may be ruined, so we may read the myth of Arthur, knowing how very true it is to the life of our imaginations.

There would be a day—there must be a day—when [Arthur] would come back to Gramarye with a new Round Table which had no corners, just as the world had none—a table without boundaries between the nations who would sit to feast there.
—T. H. WHITE
20th-century novelist, from
The Once and Future King

7

The Quest for Proof

As the legend of Arthur lives on, the search for proof of his existence continues. A great deal is known about the history of Britain just prior to Arthur's time, but written historical sources on the Age of Arthur are sketchy. Another method of discovering the distant past is by studying the physical remains of those who lived during the time. Archeologists dig up and try to understand the remnants of these earlier civilizations. By piecing together bones and those artifacts that have survived the assaults of time — odd scraps of jewelry, weaponry, pottery, stonework, and coins — they can infer a great deal about how the people in a society lived.

There is little for archeologists to work with when studying the civilization of Arthur's Britain. For unlike the Romans who had worked with durable materials, the Britons tended to use perishable materials. Their forts and homes were built from earth and wood; their daily tools were often made from carved wood; their clothing and armor were fashioned from leather, cloth, and fur, all of which disintegrate quickly with time. Archeological finds from this era include a few swords of iron; buckles, pins, shields, and helmets of brass; as well as some

> *Yet some men say in many parts of England that King Arthur is not dead, . . .and men say that he shall come again and he shall win the Holy Cross.*
> —SIR THOMAS MALORY
> 15th-century British
> writer, from *Morte d'Arthur*

Glastonbury Abbey in southwestern England. In the 12th century when King Henry II learned that King Arthur might have been buried in the abbey, excavations were conducted and the remains of Arthur and Guinevere were said to have been uncovered.

rare pieces of jewelry. For the most part archeologists studying the Age of Arthur have been rather discouraged.

One of the earliest searches for physical proof of Arthur was done in the 12th century upon the suggestion of King Henry II. During his reign there was a rumor in the western regions of Britain that the town of Glastonbury was in fact the resting place of King Arthur, the legendary Isle of Avalon, and that the great king's tomb was somewhere between two pillars in the cemetery of Glastonbury Abbey. The noted Arthurian researcher Geoffrey Ashe states that similar to many of the legends that had become prevalent since the time of Arthur, the area, "almost surrounded by marshes and lagoons, was then more or less an island in wet weather."

Henry had Glastonbury's monks begin a search for this tomb. According to Ashe, not much was done for a few years, and then the abbey burned down in 1184. The king planned for its rebuilding, and in 1190, after the king had already died, a tomb was said to have been found. A monk of the time wrote: "Seven feet down the diggers found a slab of stone and a lead cross inscribed *HIC IACET SE-PULTUS INCLITUS REX ARTURIUS IN INSULA AVALONIA*: Here lies buried the renowned King Arthur in the Isle of Avalon. Nine feet below these objects, they unearthed a huge coffin made of a hollowed oak log, embedded in the soil at a slight angle. Inside was the skeleton of a tall man, the skull damaged, also some slighter bones with a scrap of yellow hair, presumably the remains of Arthur's queen."

Then, says the monk Adam of Domerham, writing a century later, "The Abbot and the convent, raising up the remains, joyfully translated them into the great church, placing them in a double tomb, magnificently carved. The King's body was set by itself at the head of the tomb, that of the queen at the foot or the eastern part, and there remains to the present day."

The 13th-century monk goes on to say that his king, "the Lord Edward [I] . . . with his consort, the Lady Eleanor, came to Glastonbury . . . to celebrate

Easter. . . . The following Tuesday . . . at dusk, the lord king had the tomb of the famous King Arthur opened. Wherein, in two caskets painted with their pictures and arms, were found separately the bones of the said king, which were of great size, and those of Queen Guinevere, which were of marvellous beauty. . . . On the following day . . . the lord king replaced the bones of the king and those of the queen, each in their own casket, having wrapped them in costly silks. When they had been sealed they ordered the tomb to be placed forthwith in front of the high altar, after the removal of the skulls for the veneration of the people."

The markings for the location of the second tomb were discovered in 1931. The tomb as well as the rest of the abbey, however, had been destroyed in the Protestant Reformation of the 16th century. The bones supposed to be those of Arthur and his queen have never been recovered.

There is much debate over the authenticity of the tomb of Arthur. One argument states with great accuracy that a lock of human hair could not have endured over a period of 600 years; therefore, the blond hair originally recorded could not have existed. More, the lead cross that was found marking the location of the burial place, which has also been lost, is thought to have actually been made by the Glastonbury monks in order to give more credence

The 500-foot-high Glastonbury Tor (or hill) is topped by a small chapel. Associations with King Arthur abound in the legends of the tor. Some say it was here that Arthur stormed a castle in order to rescue his kidnapped queen. In fact, archeological investigation has proven the existence of a 6th-century hillfort on the tor.

to their find and thus gain greater glory for their abbey. The debate about Arthur's tomb has still not been settled and it cannot be satisfactorily established that he and his queen were ever buried at

There remains the question of fabled Camelot. Was there such a place? Recent excavations at Cadbury-Camelot, as the site in Somerset is called, seem to provide an affirmative answer to the question, though we must sadly discard any notion of plumed knights clanking about great medieval battlements.

—JUSTINE DAVIS RANDERS-
PEHRSON
American historian

Glastonbury.

In order to achieve some degree of success in the exploration of Arthur's Age, some have attempted to draw conclusions from the barest of earthen im-

An ivory chest from 14th-century France engraved with scenes from Arthurian romances. Archeological finds connected with Arthur are often not restricted to just Britain.

The sign reads:

SITE OF KING ARTHUR'S TOMB.
IN THE YEAR 1191 THE BODIES' OF
KING ARTHUR AND HIS QUEEN WERE
SAID TO HAVE BEEN FOUND ON THE
SOUTH SIDE OF THE LADY CHAPEL.
ON 19TH APRIL 1278 THEIR REMAINS WERE
REMOVED IN THE PRESENCE OF
KING EDWARD I AND QUEEN ELEANOR
TO A BLACK MARBLE TOMB ON THIS SITE.
THIS TOMB SURVIVED UNTIL THE
DISSOLUTION OF THE ABBEY IN 1539

Supposed site of King Arthur's tomb at Glastonbury Abbey. Constructed in black marble in 1278 according to the wishes of King Edward I and Queen Eleanor, the double tomb was said to contain the remains of King Arthur and Queen Guinevere.

prints left from the 6th century. The most celebrated example of this technique was the archeological search for Arthur's castle, Camelot, in South Cadbury, Somerset, England. Between 1966 and 1972, the Camelot Research Committee, co-founded by Geoffrey Ashe, discovered markings denoting the existence of an elaborate hill-fort. Enormous concentric rings of earthen embankments covering over 18 acres outlined a fortification that only a powerful warlord would have maintained. Unearthed artifacts enabled the searchers to determine that the "castle" was very active in the 6th century. The archeologists located holes dug in specific areas of the compound that once held support posts for vast timber buildings. The architectural style strongly resembled those of Roman forts that were seen in Britain just prior to the Arthurian Age. Although all the indicators gave evidence that the fort was utilized during the time of Arthur, there was no find that positively proved that Arthur had lived there.

Beyond these two debatable "Arthurian sites" are numerous places to which Arthur's name has come to be associated. The most prominent of these is Tintagel in Cornwall. At this cliff-top castle, later turned into a monastery, Arthur was said to have been conceived and born. Underneath this castle is an enormous cavern, which has come to be called Merlin's Cave. More carved places in the area are called Arthur's Chair, Arthur's Quoit (stone circle), and even Arthur's Cups and Saucers. Other areas of Cornwall have taken the names Arthur's Chair and Oven, Arthur's Hall, Arthur's Bed, and Arthur's Hunting Seat. Numerous pools are all considered by local folk to have been the body of water into which Arthur's sword Excalibur was thrown when it was returned to the Lady of the Lake.

Wales, the last refuge of the Britons, is also the home of many topographical Arthurian sites. In this land a gap between two mountains is called Arthur's Seat. A bowl-shaped rock has been dubbed Arthur's Pot, where the wizard Merlin supposedly cooked for the king. Numerous caves house sleeping knights of the Round Table, who, according to Welsh legend, will remain in that state until they hear their call to

> *And some people say that King Arthur died, and that the three Queens took his body to a little hermitage near Glastonbury, where it was buried in a chapel. But many men think that King Arthur never died at all, but dwells now in some beautiful valley of rest, and that one day he will come again to rule over England. For on his tomb this verse is written: "Here lies Arthur, King that was, and King that shall be."*
> —MARY MACLEOD
> 20th-century novelist, from
> *King Arthur and his Knights*

Sir Mortimer Wheeler, president of the Camelot Research Committee, examines an artifact unearthed at Cadbury Hill in Somerset, southwestern England, in 1966. It was here that Sir Mortimer and Geoffrey Ashe, who chronicled the committee's archeological digs, believed Camelot to have existed.

arms. Scattered stones marked by hoofprints now bear titles relating to the mounted Arthur slaying any variety of monsters. Almost every Welsh county has some Arthurian site associated with it. Each site maintains its legends, as people from each area want to have some special bond with the greatest of all kings.

But why should Arthur — border chief or mythical king — continue to fascinate so many people? Each successive age has retold the story of Arthur and used it to embody its own values. Without changing the major events in Arthur's life, so clear and fixed, well-known now after so many tellings, authors of every age provide motives and meanings significant for their own times.

The Welsh border chieftain Arthur originally survived through history by luck. For reasons we will never know for sure, the Arthur of history attracted the notice of his contemporaries and of the generations that followed. Wandering bards and writers of historical chronicles embellished his legend. Eventually King Arthur and his court acted as a magnet for all of the wonderful stories of his time. Arthur has continued to survive into the 20th century because we find in his life and court a representation of our own dreams and struggles.

Suppose Arthur had not become the center of the hopes and fears of the people of the Middle Ages? What would the difference be? Arthur would have remained just a 6th-century Welsh border chieftain, holding out against the inevitable Anglo-Saxon conquest. His name would have been remembered only by a few historians who studied that shadowy period, and by the people of Wales and other areas of western England, who might have considered him a local hero. But the story of Arthur took a different turn, and it is we who stand enriched by a tale of magical castles, enchanted forests, the beautiful queen, the Holy Grail, Excalibur, the Round Table, Camelot, Avalon, and above all Arthur — most human of heroes, at once so powerful, so decisive, so just, and yet, when all is said and done, so alone, so vulnerable, so much like ourselves — the once and future king.

T. H. White, the author of the popular work *The Once and Future King*, is often considered responsible for the resurgence of interest in King Arthur that occurred during the mid-20th century.

King Arthur (center) as depicted in a 12th-century Italian mosaic. As the Arthurian
legend continued to spread
throughout the world, the
tale became less a part of
the history of Britain and
more a story of chivalry.

Further Reading

Alcock, Leslie. *Arthur's Britain.* London: The Penguin Press, 1971.

Briggs, Asa. *A Social History of England.* New York: Viking, 1984.

Laing, Lloyd. *Celtic Britain.* New York: Charles Scribner's Sons, 1979.

Loomis, Roger Sherman. *The Development of Arthurian Romance.* New York: W. W. Norton Co., Inc., 1963.

Malory, Sir Thomas. *The Works of Sir Thomas Malory.* London: Oxford University Press, 1954.

Morris, John. *The Age of Arthur.* London: Weidenfield and Nicolson, 1973.

Morris, Rosemary. *The Character of King Arthur in Medieval Literature.* Cambridge: Brewer, 1982.

Tatlock, J. S. P. *The Legendary History of Britain.* Berkeley: University of California Press, 1950.

Tennyson, Alfred Lord. *Idylls of the King.* New York: New American Library, 1961.

Welch, George Patrick. *Britannia.* Middletown: Wesleyan University Press, 1963.

White, T. H. *The Once and Future King.* New York: G. P. Putnam's Sons, 1965.

Chronology

410	The Visigoth leader, Alaric, captures Rome; Rome is no longer able to protect Britain
c. 450	Anglo-Saxons begin to gain control of England
c. 475	Birth of Arthur
c. 517	Arthur defeats the Saxon forces at the Battle of Badon
c. 538	Arthur is killed at the Battle of Camlann
597	Augustine of Canterbury begins the Christianization of England
c. 600	Anglo-Saxons control almost all of Great Britain
	The *Gododdin*, a poem containing the first mention of Arthur, is composed
c. 800	Welsh historian Nennius writes *History of Britain*, crediting Arthur with leading a number of British victories, including the Battle of Badon
	Start of the Viking conquest of England
871–79	Reign of Alfred the Great; peace with the Vikings
1066	Norman conquest of England
1137	Geoffrey of Monmouth compiles *The History of the Kings of Britain*, which popularizes Arthur's legend
1190	A tomb reputed to be Arthur and Guinevere's is found in Glastonbury
c. 1470	Sir Thomas Malory writes *Morte d'Arthur (The Death of Arthur)*
1859–85	Alfred, Lord Tennyson, writes *Idylls of the King*

Index

Paul C. Doherty is Associate Professor of English at Boston College, and formerly served as chair of the English department and Associate Dean of the college. He lives in Newton Centre, Massachusetts, with his wife and three children.

Arthur M. Schlesinger, jr., taught history at Harvard for many years and is currently Albert Schweitzer Professor of the Humanities at City University of New York. He is the author of numerous highly praised works in American history and has twice been awarded the Pulitzer Prize. He served in the White House as special assistant to Presidents Kennedy and Johnson.